T0103944

BEJEWELED

POETRY

Revelations
Sensations
Creations

M. JEWEL H.

Order this book online at www.trafford.com
or email orders@trafford.com

Most Trafford titles are also available at major online book retailers.

Printed in the United States of America.

ISBN: 978-1-4907-3045-5 (sc)
ISBN: 978-1-4907-3046-2 (hc)
ISBN: 978-1-4907-3050-9 (e)

Library of Congress Control Number: 2014904768

Trafford rev. 03/13/2014

www.trafford.com

North America & international
toll-free: 1 888 232 4444 (USA & Canada)
fax: 812 355 4082

Contents

Revelations Sensations Creations

Revelations unexpected understandings developing the
continuity of the self
Reaching newfound depths embodying a richness of wealth
Symbolic of the connectivity
Disparate remnants left
From germinating seedlings of Insight

Tonight

Sensations romanticizing every tenuous extended fingertip to the
endearing touch enough to grasp the entire beings embodiment
A glance through the masses that envelopes an eternity of
sentiments
Breathing intertwined entering minds ecstatically elegant
Always

Today

Creations trifecta tiers of unity
Resonate invincibly scribed dutifully
Apex, base, core integrally
Demonstrative structures arise beautifully
A conscious exclamation in light

LIFE

Verse is Solace

Verse is Solace
The devoted listening ear of the page
The immense truth of the pen
Creates the wise adage

Verse is comfort
The exacting rhythms of heart
Pour into penmanship unrelenting
Allows healing to start

Verse is kind
Non-judgmental, receptive and fair
Key in the reasons the questions the seasons
Crafty understanding will be there

Verse is omniscient
In ethereal breaths spoken or whimsical thought
Conjure the flow that is beautiful to know
There is nowhere that it is not

Verse is peace
No trials no consternation no hurry
Always patient ever transient unpretentious no worries

Verse is Love
It is not self seeking it is never demeaning or strife
To the paper to the screen to the ink or the ream let it flow
Verse is Life

Revelations

I'm a lot tougher than I thought
I am stronger than I know
My own power I must've forgot
I am my own hero

I have more conviction than I had counted
I have more fortitude than I first knew
I'm focused in a direction that amounts to
I am my own rescue

I am more creative than I had imagined
I am wiser than I had surmised
I am more skillful than I had challenged
I am my own surprise

I am more beautiful than I had noticed
I am bold without hesitation
I am more suitable to the supernatural
I am my own inspiration

An extraordinary woman looked up at me
I was captivated and I drew nearer
To admire her features her grace her face
I saw her in the mirror

An exceptional woman spoke to me
I was intrigued and I took notes
To her poetry it was notably
The most profound thing I ever wrote

An effervescent woman presented to me
By her energy I was enamored
Her excitement transpired her charisma entirely complimented
her Glamour

A clairvoyant woman grasped my hand And recited assuredly
and calm
A buoyant future although I barely knew her
Ascension inscribed in my Palm

It is with no doubt I move forward
It is myself I found in separations
To success and wonder I dedicatedly commit
As I witness and write
Revelations

No Misunderstanding My Love

Into the intricacies of my sensory
Attuned to the ephemeral of my understanding
All nuances of cross syllogistic epistemology
Our hearts meet our spirits dancing

Beyond realms of interscopic intransience
Into depths of amalgamative wonder
Cinch throws of tectonic power abodes
Creating lightening, resounding thunder

Formative night skies consubstantial with the Father
Elegant earthscapes And junoesque harbors
Ethereal lands regenerate retreating arbors
Unveiling it's brocade of love

Together unalienated service
Lends charity to preordinate worship
Never turning it's back wouldn't hurt it, esteemed adorned
And forever perfect

Enter indelible enlightening whims
A measure together is undeniably him
Defiantly architect the elation from grim
Subcutaneously project the gentle prism

To reflect essential sensual thrones
To connect individuals predominately postponed
To select incinerated hypothalmic moans
Prophylactically own

No misunderstanding my love

The resources of peace bespeak of
Eviscerating the confides destruction
Permitting communicates to illuminate the inordinate disclosure
Above

Reciting real reel real are the heavens
Awnings unlatched read the score
Victorious is the upward story of the amorous team heretofore

Paranormal Paramour

Supernatural opining paramour
Overzealous spiritual resident
The medium will not close the habitation not disposed
Typical spiritual elements

Present the paranormal clinching covetousness and keeping
Parasitic on carriers and preselected listeners riding speaking
feeding

Breeding into existence
The transcripts interlocutory share
Envious of sins of such mortals
Symptoms and strategies aware . . .

Aware of unearthly brooding
Unchanged by metaphysical doings
Captive the conscious splitting vortex
Hauntings rantings and enchanting spewing

Speak whisper let it flow
This vacuous template greets
And welcomes the longings straining to impart
And artistry and aesthetics meet

Plotting against the palpable
Pranks against the pleased
Entertaining a while
Unchaining unrivaled cadences insatiably appeased

Disrupting damaging primordial relationships
Replacing with eternal devotions
Sentiments succumb to immutable the one of ephemeral
emotions

Cryptic courtship proceeds
And angelic ciphers commence
Humanity collapses at the feet of the entrapment of epic
connections and extraterrestrial events

Deal

You're ideal
For me
You've captured my attention
At this interval nothing more
Than to be in your dimension

You're wonderful
In your own way
Exactly what excites
Me releasing free
Is righteous and delights

You're only
The one
That I desire and nothing more
Its beyond any behavior or favors before

You love me
Very truly yours am I
Time can only fill with more affection as I try

To let you know
I love you
And it took no time to be real
It is the ultimate merger
Deal.

No Deal

You require everything
And offer nothing
And wonder why
I cannot

You challenge reality
And offer no fantasy
And are confused
Because I will not

You disrupt the established
And offer no alternative
And ponder
While I forgot

There is no deal
When the circumstance are so real
And the parameters are illogical
There is no love to feel

That strong
It is only wrong
To consider me
For you

Mosaic

Once upon a time
beautiful reflection
gentle engraved cameo portrait
Shattered in a wave of
Carelessness, disregard
and coarseness

Litany of shards
Unguarded forcefulness
Splintering elegance
Remorseless

Lining the unclear passageway
Unexpectant disbursement
Caustically

Rummaging riders trample
With hooves and wheels
Glasslike crumbles
Fragments still
Resembles the original in multiples
Stronger smaller as steel

Multicolored from trolling
Villagers, visitors, villains trace
Multitextured from pillagers wanderers and chased
Multidimensional essential when the world is erased
A mosaic multitiered in the window is placed

A mosaic multipurpose
Captures the suns wide array
A mosaic multi-instructional
Describes ancient days
A mosaic multi-institutional sheds diversity of lights on
adversity's ways
Luminosity is right in cathedrals unshaded
The ferocity of love is all colors and all lovers unhated
The penetration of light through the restructured reflection
Exceptionally immaculate elevation
Mosaic

Disarming

Silence is golden
Because your darkness disarms me
Maybe because you are as meticulous as a seasoned surgeon
And powerful as the kings triumphant army

You deliver life into this world
Making my machinations conceive
The fanciful handsome beautiful expandable
Mustard seeds in which I believe

Threatening mutual assured blessed deconstruction for which
you will never pull the trigger
My ally, my Jedi, my frontline, my medi, my ace, my
constellation, my winner

My scripture I'm writing
My measurement of timing
My masterpiece defining
A man
Encased in epoch midnight enshrining intricacies of an
irretrievable plan

Tonight my guard has fallen
Last night my sword and shield too
Dissolved in rain of the imminent domain of the
Excellence of me and you
Together

There were no weary on the field there were no cowards
in the helm
The flag was raised it traveled up mountainous terrain
for days and at the victors feet befell

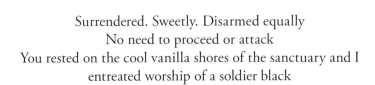

Surrendered. Sweetly. Disarmed equally
No need to proceed or attack
You rested on the cool vanilla shores of the sanctuary and I
entreated worship of a soldier black

BLACKOUT

(Disclaimer: I truly do, love every hue, but for the few here I acknowledge and express an endearing love)

If you weren't so Black
I wouldn't want you back
Legacy strong
Emphatically belong
If you weren't such a man
I would've made other plans
But you are
And by far
I love your time
How you enter
How you arrive
Intimate closeness
Inner thigh
You're so Black
I love that
I dream of you
In my room white therein
Intoxicated by your complexion
How could I not be overcome by you in the night
A thousand ways
The face
The body
Holding black back
Lifting up
Black gentle black rough
Never enough
So Black

In the Dark
He stole my heart
Now I can never be
Torn apart

From him
I imagine
His arms
His charm
His grin

I require
I desire
I admire
I win

I hope
I devote
I evoke
I begin

I inhale, I exhale
I wait, I count
I hunger, I wonder
I break, I shout

I Blackout
I pass out
I fall out
I freeze

So hot
I cannot
Get out of bed
Or off my knees praying for your life, safety, sanity
Black is humanity
Once not considered so
Black flesh bleeds red blood too
with blue veins to a heart go

I endear a color
It is every array in one
It is everything
It is pleasing
It is Black Addiction

If you weren't so Black
I wouldn't know all of that
If you weren't so strong
I wouldn't know how to get along
If you weren't such a man
I wouldn't understand
Chasing

But you are

So Black
I love that
Everything about me craves
Everything black about you
I wait for night everyday

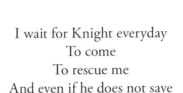

I wait for Knight everyday
To come
To rescue me
And even if he does not save
I still fall at his feet

Black
King
Black
Court
Black
Right
Black
Report

I want blackened salmon
I write in black ink too
Black labels black tables
Chocolate tiramisu

I want mahogany accents
And dark oak hardwood floors
I want deep smooth finish leather inside
& midnight exterior

I want to go to the continent
black packs black racks black hole
Black pursuits black troops
Black roots Black songs black
Soul

I want to paint black with my fingers
I want to walk at dusk at night
I love to see black beauty
I'm impartial to the light

I want to cook and kindle
To warm hearts in hearth black
I love that Black too resembles in its image the Creator and love
attracts

Hair like sheep's wool
Feet like copper
Can't stop her
she washes his feet
He bears his cross no time is lost
He walks in Destiny to meet
Black height
On a hill
The black wood
Black blood spills
The black sky
covers now
The black wreath
Thorns
Black head bow
The black stone
Positioned back
The black death sentence obtained
Overcome by the Love of One
All of the Earth Changed

So Black
I love that
Black Benevolent Men
Black enchanting surface
Black victorious win

Black so endless
Black magnetic skin
Black and forth
From darkness all begin

Deep voice
Intellect
Cool demeanor
Greatest depth
Righteous please
Quiet needs
Strong faith
Good deeds

So Black
I love that
To Black
I ode
I oath
I owe

To Black
I adore at
All times
I need
I know

For your
Blackness may
Endowment always stay
None can remove the ways

Your darkness leaves an impression on me
Truly
I neither can nor want to escape
The Night of you
Is so right Allelujah

I just want to participate
Let me
Love you
Back
Let me
Love you
Black

Eternally
No worries
No doubt
I exist because of your love
black kiss black wish black list black this is a
BLACKOUT

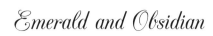

Emerald and Obsidian

Emerald green and Lucite, precious and rare of worth
Obsidian black and smooth refined from molten rock of earth

Princess cut and set in modern
Casing to be adorned
Harvested volcanic removal from ash both celebrated and
mourned

Clarity like clairvoyance lending visions into the vast
Night and dark so poignant depicting genesis past

Green like the tender leaf
Unbent, untouched, unchanging
Black projecting strength so solid so stone so amazing

The Emerald gleam is palatable sparkles in Sun and moonlight
Obsidian of dreams admirable coarse to spark and ignite

Of the earth formations
Still beams constellation up above
The Emerald and Obsidian compliment and firmament the
ornament
Of Love

Own It

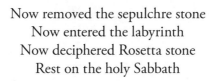

Now removed the sepulchre stone
Now entered the labyrinth
Now deciphered Rosetta stone
Rest on the holy Sabbath

Now untraced the fragile linen
Now stomped the grapes of wrath
Now poured forgiveness, sinless, win this like no other hath

Now impaled the intractable beast
Now traveled unraveled entrails
Now sifted the sands of unconquerable lands
Lift the glory veil

Now entwined gilded threads of mind
Now tenuously completed the garment
Now demonstrated your skillful willful design
Present at a pinnacle
No one can harm it

Bow down before your diadem
Prostrate and release your tools
Ignobly refrain All things have changed and
Genuflect before your jewel

Its yours
You earned it
Cherish it
Keep it
Yours
You deserve it
Love it
Treat it
Ours
You worked it
Adore it
Reach it

The seed
you've dutifully sown it
Is all for you entirely precious
True
Now you
Own it

Just Dessert

A honey kiss chocolate truffle bliss cherries jubilee
Merlot drizzled splendor
A fondant shaved confectioned glazed caramel sauce pecan
dipped fudge melting heart wonder

Paired with a Rose' refreshingly light hints of berries fresh from
the vine spun
Tantalizing tastes to satiate the palate and bubbles to tickle the
tongue

Dessert before dinner at night
Dessert as breakfast by day
Dessert lunch
Dessert brunch
Dessert presented a multitude of ways

Leaven rising mixtures to oven
Set marinating glazes until midnight
Ingredients stir added love folded in
Recipes creations from adaptations alright

Dessert take to work
Take Dessert breaks
Dessert domestic or internationally far
Dessert illuminates and ingratiates darkness
Dessert institutes subversion of entrees five star

Dessert after long trying days
Dessert on rainy cold nights
Dessert inspired consequentially
Nourishes and delights

In Decadence indulge
Shamelessly
In deliciousness enjoy endless
A tapestry of elegant pastry, bakery, making healthy rich and
guiltless

Awakening tastebuds insatiable
Satisfying cravings discreet and covert
Flaunting fetishes red velvet rum cinnamon cacao vanilla
coconut chocolate lime divine
Just desserts

My Everything Yours

My Heartbeat-Yours
Steps of my Feet-Yours
Across an Ocean-Yours
Total Devotion-Yours

My Spine-Yours
My Time-Yours
Earth Rotation-Yours
That Elevation-Yours

That axis-Yours
That access-Yours
That practice-Yours
Them taxes-Yours

That tipping-Yours
That missing-Yours
Ears listening-Yours
All wishing-Yours

My deepest-Yours
My weakness-Yours
My birthday-Yours
My worst way-Yours

My very best-Yours
Every Next-Yours
That house built-Yours
That outfield-Yours
That infield-Yours
That instilled-Yours
Enigmatic-Yours
Systematic-Yours

Boat docks-Yours
Photos, shop-Yours
That turntable-Yours
Exclusive Labels-Yours

In my eyes blink consider more
Ways that I think I'm Yours
My breath-to you
What I do-for you

My all-Yes
My call-Yes
When it rains it Pours
My Everything
Yours

Basic

In the most basic of interactions
In the most trying time of need
We realized in revelation
That love can succeed

In the mire of humanity
In the trials of ailing and strife
We realized emphatically
That's my love for life

In the shadows of the season
In the pain of prolonged travail
We epitomized a sweet reality
Removed from facades veil

It was only in incapacity
It was only near entrapped
Did All walls come down all pretense drowned
All the magic happened

I could pin you a halo
And you forge me wings that night
Never two more equal people
In more innocent connectivity invite

I could address an audience
As I could whisper my soul
You could pronounce in bravado your most clandestine
annotations scrolled

It read love me love me love me
Please love me forever and a day
It was in the silence and the softest touch
Joined together us for always

In the Deep

I'm out here in the deep
I've gone too far from land
Far in the deep end
Without barge or brink or sand
(. . . was gone to meet a man)
Its dark here in the deep
The ocean waves surround
The crests splash the monotonous motions roll
Its a wonder I have not drowned
I cling tightly to
Thoughts of me and you
It propels and keeps me afloat
As I drift in this channel
Trying to get a handle on the
Love boat

I want to know Love
Want it to pick me up want it to come by here
I'm so far out in the deep
It may pass me by I fear

So I send up a signal
With my heart and call out from down my spine
I shine my light I blow my whistle I try to influence matter with
mind
I try to pass the time
It seems that the ocean is aligned to win
In this vast sea against little me
Out here in the deep end
Past where seagulls bother to belly past where doves branches
send
Love alone keeps me
Each new day begin

With hope and understanding
And new ways to adore
Just to soak in someone's silence and not demanding more
Just to gaze into the same sky I know my lover sees
The moonlight that shines upon him somewhere is the same that
shines on me
The stars that set in constellation are the same alignment to both
our eyes,
Aquarius, Sagittarius, Scorpio, Taurus, Virgo, Gemini
The same cold wind somewhere brushes him and then begins to
be my breeze
The same air that keeps me alive travels to him that he also
breathes
The same thought crosses both of our minds at some time and I
am pleased
The same cross is lifted somewhere on earth and both of our
burdens are eased
This has to be love I presume
And delight as I exhume its ways
Out in the deep great company I keep with my open heart as it
pounds and it prays
This is falling in love I believe
And I'm amused as I assume its
Plans
Out in the deep daydreaming of sleeping right next to my man
This is honoring love I know
And I'm humbled by its power
Out in the deep unsurrounded to keep focus minute to minute
and hour to hour
Each passing time
Solely reminds me of the omniscience
Love is real
Real love is deep
God is Love
Ubiquitous

Unresponsive

His heart stopped
Beating
For me, days and days ago
His Mind stopped
Thinking
Of me, thoughts of me no more
His body stopped
Responding
To me, His feeling let go
Unresponsive the status
The diagnosis
Comatose

Sustained on life support
To ease the burden of tragedy
In hopes of vitality
In patience for a remedy

Progressive science
Aggressive alternatives
Holistic wellness
Equally fail
Now at the hospice chaplain
To the resident deacon
Tell

Over
Death of relationship
Here fearing the worst
Perhaps seeking comfort
In prayer where
It hurts

Loss of a life
With another
That cannot be sustained
Moments seemingly immeasurable
Emotionally drained

Physically neglected
Mentally racked
Love has left
And I just want my love back

Still I Miss You

Seems like all signs point
To the end of the road
I've already lamented descent from my future goals
It feels like I'm laying on the bottom of the floor with an
improbable load, to lift
And still I want you

Seems like all arrows lead to an empty place
I have no shame in saying
I want to see your face
I've already sacrificed reservations, pace
It won't quit and I admit
I still miss you

Seems like all sands have run through the hour glass
I must admit time seems like it can never pass
In your absence I just want to be free at last, and that
Is to kiss you

The DJ can't play me a song
There are no words or tunes to help me get along
I've resorted to the melody that my heart beats on
Mixed with breaths that says he left and exhalation that say he's
gone

The better part of me believes there is a greater fix
In moments to come we'll Look and laugh at all of this
Just like when I said I'd been so long uninspired till on your bed
Where we laid as the rain coated the skyscapes in a wintry mix

I look whole but I have empty holes
I sound optimistic but I have challenged goals
Its almost a new era
What does the future hold?
You're not here but it's like your near and
Still I miss you

Silence

Silence
Dealt
Its didactic
Blow
Mindblowing
Felt
Its turbulent
Woe
Quiet
Resonance
Distance
Grow
Disruption
Distraction
Boredom
Slow
Silence
Smacked
Its humbling
Pound
Reverberate
Shock
The only
Sound
Pressure
The absence
Left
All around

No one
Looked
Nothing
Found
All hidden
Inside
Wept
Numb
Dumb
Silence
Kept

Concession

Concede defeat
Exit race
Throw in towel
Didn't place

Accept loss
Acknowledge fail
Admit over
End trail

Game over
Notice played
Final score
Not delayed

No challenges left
Ruling stands
No time on clock
No loyal fans

Trophy never
Crown not
Medal not even
All forgot

No handshake
No nod
No pat on the back
No explanation
No hesitation
No rolling tape back

No review
No reward
No prize
No money
No certificate
No honorary mention
No honey
No sugar
No bite
No kiss
No text
No missing
No speaking
No listening
No next
No date
No need to wait
No call
No come
No faking
No trip taking
No fun
Just done

No hugs
No hi's
No lows
No where to go
No goodbyes
No holding
No folding

No checking
No catch
No messing
No pressing
No guessing
No match
No care
No share
No cuddle
No keep
No late night
No early morning
No breakfast
No sleep
No lips
No hips
No stares
No eyes
No wonder
No wander
No caress
No thigh
No breast
No body
No touch
No taste
No lunch
No friend
No feeling
No taste
Nada

Nothing
Zip
Zilch
Zero
Never
Ever
Not even a no

That's it
No more
Its a rap
Bell ringing
Lady singing
Loud Fat

Curtains
Closed
No encore no clapping
Joke
Bombed
Nobody
Laughing

Nothing happening
Shut Down
Concede
Must have been
Not meant to be

The Heartbreaker Cannot Heal

Now I'm suffocating
And he won't give me mouth to mouth
He won't deliver compressions to my heart
And he's letting me bleed out

I've been cut so deeply
I can't suppress the wound
An artery connected straight to my heart
This love is doomed

He won't bandage what is broken
Shattered in many places
Immovable and do you know
He provides no splints or braces

No crutches lent to lean upon
No ventilation for my breathing
No ace bandage no cold turkey sandwich
No help, no heal, no feeding

Pain killers must be placebo
The sharpness won't go numb
The aching hasn't subsided
Ohhh this thought is dumb . . . because

The perpetrator will not save you
The rescuer will not come
The inflictor of the trauma
Is Not the one
Who can help you as you suffer
Indifference to your state
The binder of the broken hearted is Never the one who breaks

No Less

I should've left in the pouring rain
Now I'm looking for a window to get out
No one could contemplate or appreciate my pain
Or the reason my soul needs to shout

I should've left you in the pouring rain
But your lack of substance doesn't make me less faithful
Your lack of trust doesn't make make me less noble
and your lack of strength doesn't make me less able

I should've left in the pouring rain
But your poor decisions
Make me no less wise
Your frequent revisions make me no less perfect
Your heartlessness
Won't make me cry

I should've left you in the pouring rain
In your pathetic heat and desperation
Because you would heal with actions unreal
A cold unfeeling separation

I could have left you
Life on the line
But I have not loss my favor
I have not emptied my compassion
I have not tapered my behavior

I could have turned away
And immediately ran
But stayed and cared
Demonstrated love for a man

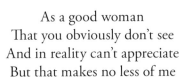

As a good woman
That you obviously don't see
And in reality can't appreciate
But that makes no less of me

I should've left in the pouring rain
But I ain't scared of no weather
and if you were fearless too
Honestly we could have been together

Heart Wise

My heart asks me listen
It implores I consider how it beats
Painting a perfect vision
Of you
And me

My heart is indicting a good matter
Interject God in Permanency
To a relationship built on trust
And love and hope truly

My heart it speaks the truth
My heart is deaf to my mind
My heart requires no proof
My heart keeps not track of day or time

My heart only knows you
To communicate all I do
Is commune with my heart
Which is yours and mine belongs to you

In quietness and confidence
My strength
My dream come true
The sky the limit
Loving hearts free
Nothing can undo

Or restrain or tame or keep
Sweethearts sweet devotion
Not wild horses not obstacle courses, sand, or land or ocean

My hearts desire
That I know
With certainty of the law
And compliance to nature
Science and spiritual
To disregard what I saw
Forget what I have heard
And ignore the facts and figures
And just trust in His word

Love bears all things
Believes all things
Love catches you when you fall
Love cares for you
Love heals
Love conquers all

My heart loves
Mighty conqueror
My heart owes
All glory and praise
To the most high
For you and I
In love always

My heart is pure and precious
In the matters that I keep
Upon my bed
Tonight I Wed
Autonomous when I sleep
still beats for you
Without conscious thought or trying
My heart beats in continual perfect timing

It prevents me from dying
It needs no guidance it is wise
It loves on
It beats strong
It's never wrong
I realized

Pleading

I've been wrongly convicted
And am now serving an inglorious sentence
Incommensurate to any crime I'm innocent and begrudge my
unnecessary penance

I've been falsely accused
and I'm a victim of biased judgment
I have been by injustice wronged and bruised and don't feel I
deserve this punishment

False witnesses slander my good name
And the malevolent fiercely betray
they seek my ruin but can't be my undoing
I enter this pleading today

Consider my character henceforth
Contemplate my countless good deeds
Carefully recount my actions amount to
The appeal for special proceedings I plead

Vacate the motion in error
Immediately move to dismiss
Release her in bondage for restoration of homage and surely
sanctity remit

I am not a villain
You cannot prosecute me
Of treachery, adultery, larceny,
Manslaughter or treason
I am not guilty

I am not guilty
I lack the requisite mental state
No mens rea for what the say I've done
They indict me with nothing but hate

I am not guilty
Virtuous and true
I lack the requisite intent
No harm I have meant
No reproachable deed I would do

Especially to you
He who my mind thinks of
He who my heart longs for
He who my body does love

Wholly innocent
And if there was a smear would repent for it
And if ever drew a tear would condemn the flow of it
And if otherwise did declare would just admit to it

Totally innocent
Not insecure, also hardly hesitant
Still sincere always endearing also still very relevant

Take away
This unfortunate pronouncement
Vacay this order that contemptuous assails
May the good fellow that I came to know find wisdom to lead a
righteous heart to be redeemed and prevail!

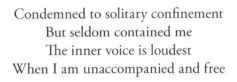

Solitary Escape

Condemned to solitary confinement
But seldom contained me
The inner voice is loudest
When I am unaccompanied and free

Almost exhausting listening yet still the words I do heed
Clear the insight diligently I write and receive and need

The voice speaks fire in absence and overflows like pouring rain
Of blood from
From an aortic vein or valve directly out of my heart cut pain

Hemorrhaging out all that is inside
While relegated to this space
Insufferable moments bemoaned in a poetic way that doesn't
waste

Solitary confinement the sentence
But solitary confidement the result
the wrecking ball shifted the side planks lifted the ball dropped
making a catapult

There is a way out of this fixture
There is escape from this dungeon
The tools fastened for harm will restructure and warn there is
freedom on the horizon

The heavy sealed door will crumble
Alone by myself I can't stay
The innermost telling will defeat solemn dwellings
And propel my own get away

Escape to a new day

The inner voice freed

Joy and gratitude display

Resolution MyCare

I need to pass a clean continuing resolution
For the upcoming year
Minimize waste and excessive loopholes with romantic
discretion clear

I won't adjourn until agreeing upon an itemized guide
Leading without operating in waste
One that protects the unfortunate and one that connects the
displaced

We will work through the night for an agreement
I will personally take a stand for inclusion
Of a MyCare provision to advance without revision
To provide coverage for my ailing heart the solution

I'm confident at sessions closure
The standing bill will prove moreover
That this delegate has her needs met
For the betterment of the union
Vote her

New Nation of Celebration

I've joined the collective body of pain
By knowing sorrow
The connection garnered my admission
The induction occurs tomorrow

Raising my right hand
To affirm or Avow
Solemnly
That I can now relate
Humbly to masses
How we all suffer
Is actually great

Because the burden is light
And when shared is alright
A heavy cross only an exercise in turns
Building strength and endurance
Acquired assurance
Many hands make light work I learned

One in the body
That all share
Grievance filed my application
Remorse approved
The collective body it moved
To allow me to take a place there

A seat in place
membership and a taste
Of the bittersweet medicine a dose
Congratulatory of the misery in company and in hands glass for
a celebratory toast

I'm in the club they say
But I dont want to be that way
I'll infiltrate in the morn
Change the title of the group
and Joy recoup with gratitude in the midst of the storm

Recodify the rules
Renounce the fools
Propose a new doctrine amendment adjustments
A new constitution write a new union of the body create a new
pact and entrustment
1. Always be thankful
2. Use right what you're able
3. Ignite a spark to the dim
4. Love yourself wholly
5. Love others soulfully
6. Give as if unto yourself again and again
7. Live in light of awareness of the preciousness of health
8. Wealth is in words and learned
9. Richness is in love
10. Joy is blessings discerned

Ratify the petition,
The first in admission
To the new proposition once of the forlorn
Is an independence from tyranny of sadness the enemy and a
new nation of celebration is born!!!

Along Came Better

Along Came something better
Replacing thoughts of you
Chasing away the old and lame
Bringing something new

Incoming something awesome
Eliminating the unfit
Deciminating more excellent
Discriminating wac/legit

Ushering in the standout
Eradicating the shade
Simplifying made out
Raising a standard made

Guiding in a light
Shining like a star
Timing on point a new joint
The other won't get very far

Arising like a new dawn
Defining a new day
Alright enter Greater
And let lesser go away

Surprise see its wonderful
All eyes admire well
Desiring to be beautiful
The unfolding story tell

Passing the unfortunate
Blessing the wholly true
Creating the exceptional
Addressing me to you

Opening the written letter
Hoping that it reads
All things will forever
Be in measure to your good deeds

Explaining that which watered
Hydrating that which grown
Evading the tears cast no longer there
Reaping what has been sown

Seedling in the ground
Needing to be nourished
Taken care of now aware of
Being bountiful flourished

Along Came something Better
Actually the best
Derived from the very contents inside
Love faith works Genesis

I Still Believe in Miracles!

I still believe in Miracles!
I believe them with my soul
I see them
I receive them
I agree with them
I behold!

I must always believe in Miracles
The perfect plans evolve
The perfect time
The perfect find
The puzzling problem solved!

I will always believe in Miracles
They need no explanation
Just Happen
Laughing
Thankfully
Divine ordination

I love the Miracles
When man
No plans try to botch
Suddenly a wonderful thing happened!
If you don't believe me just watch!

Exactly at that moment
When you feel all hope is gone
Or is non-existent here comes a visit that proves
God's moves are On!!!

I still I will I shall I must
Believe in Miracles
and always trust
He who small things never fuss
And big things He takes care for us

I must I shall I will I try
Believe in Miracles
Till I die
Be thankful never asking why
He is so Miraculous
Is why we are alive

I do I do forever and a day
Believe in Miracles
Anyway
Believe in Awesome power plays
By God the Creator
of delays and raise
Friends forever
Like heart shaped clay
Kindled in hearth
To always stay
Sun in the morning
Pink orange haze
Love eternal
From crush craze
Energetic together
from listless laze

Eyes widened from shut crying
To then be amazed
Elevated from mundane
To sweetly star gaze
Exceedingly above
all that we think possible
Ever ask or imagine
Sing Praise
And worship
The starship
Has come
7 ways
Sprinkling
Blasting
Exacting
It says

Always believe in Miracles
Miracles happen everyday
Miracles are true and perfect for you
Miracles Save!!!

Scarab Soul

I am the dromedary
Of a dying artistry
Poetry
That I must bring to life

On my back strapped
Parchments intertwined
Tapestries woven
Insights

In the Sahara
A journey together
Archaic tombs once silent casings
Resurrect intersect intellect circumspect imbuement
Embalmment fading
Hierarchical chasing
Iconoclastic pacing
Monochromatic waiting

Predating penmanship promulgated by Sun reconstructing
hieroglyphic enactments to the tactic of one

The Scarab
Dutifully acquiescent does draw
The incandescent to it's ordinance in celestial position
By its durable back and intractable claws

Arise and shine
Treasure golden jewels gorgeous
Burial hoarding purporting purpose everlasting emoting

Eroded latches envisioned maps be the guidance to the optic
pyramidal temple peak
Coptic
Adopted ways casting endless
Reminiscent plays
Deciphering remnants descriptions of ways
The papyrus hewn
Exacted in Sun
Protracts the Nile dipped aortic rainbow tipped instrument
Begun
To inscribe Alive
The mysteries shunned
To liberation from hibernation
A retelling engine
Working for release
Arising a right
To everlasting dawns
From undeliverable nights
I write
The dromedary
While the weary, the catchless draw old
The witness not the matchless
The Scarab Soul

Medium

Oh how giddy
Born to amuse inspire delight
How fancy how dandy
So gleeful that I write
In abscence
Interruption of life and tedium
To lean in and made to listen
To be used as a medium

Oh how joyful
Born to entertain, interact
How wondeful or woeful
Expressions not holding back

Given an inch and taking a mile recounting long lost days
Of living and giving meter to prose that flows about in phrase

Keep me as earthly conduit
Dutifully pen recluse
This poetic conference
I attend and duties do

Keep me as connection
I will keep an open mind
And dilligently visit the poetic vortex that spans realms and time

Keep me as concubine
To the verse I am bethrothed
Knowing greatness interaction like this I vow a Medium oath

I will always want you
Write flow aloud reread
spirituals, visuals, audible
The wisdom that I need

I will always cherish you
A gift perfect impartation transfer
I will always welcome I will always adore
Ask and answer

Honored by the appointment
Graciously accept
Thankful to be considered worthy of unearthly spiritual connect

People are jealous of the prose
So attentive, inventive,
write
First thing in the morning, six times a day and then revisit at
night

The best ever
effortlessly existing engagement
Of the mind, body and conscious soul
Is metaphysical it is spiritual
It Is divine arrangement

Confluence

The rapture has come and collected
No one yet waiting on the tarp
The violins muse already concluded
Now in heavens only string the harp

Doves and ravens embattled
Purple or gold monarchy
In flight to the edge of night
Peplum peace v.s.
Bedlam anarchy

The nightwatch stands at the post
Guarded and gated assumed
Unbeknownst arrived Pandora
Be wise flora and fauna exhumed

That panda is actually a guide
That jaguar is actually the prey
The predator is a metaphor
Consumed creativity nourishes calamity

Archived tunnels transport the minions
To dominions even darker than day
Funneling out the meadows where deer and bunny rabbits play

Funny how the videos remind us of the fantasy that is not
actually
The realm we inhabit the guise a habit to expunge the cursory

Wants

Wanton carelessly thoughts
Appropriations casually forgot
A diatribe of malignant jaunts
Just to be recognized
Not even flaunt

This morning came in with a flurry
With Sun rays in the overhang still present
A confluence of the irrevocable angst ranks with the
imperturbably pleasant

Rose Grows

You present to me ill
Still I wish you well
Your penchant is mendacity
It's the truth I tell

It's this unreal

It's alright
Absence tonight
no presence today
Its too late to apologize
But I forgive you anyway

Monday morning I welcome
Sunday night I prayed
The ground was watered while storming
A beautiful rose grows always

Despite efforts to stomp
In defiance of prospects to pull
The thorns protected
The sun reflected
And now unfolds in bloom full

Beautiful
Unique
Sweet
Admired adored awaits
In carefully crafted elegance
That none unworthy can take

Phantom Feelings

This pain is Not real
I only feel
The phantom of its deleterious weight
Throbbing throughout tearless sobbing amounts solely
To a severance to which I await
Its closure

Southern Exposure
Inclement sentiments
Untraceable remnants
Suggest
An actual ache but its only
Tempest

It hovers about joints
and is uncovered by the annointing
The falsity shined upon in the light
Is just an imagery of pain
It is not sustained
And willfully will be alright

Inoperative of motive
The votive candle can be quoted
Flame steady chemically restructures the wax
From solid to melt
From bruising to welt
To healing from unannounced
Attack

Phantoms like feelings
Are intangible not real things
Unless they are believed in and kept
Otherwise feel a new way there is no existence of a heartache
And no tear trace because
Jesus wept

Sound of a Breaking Heart

What sound does a breaking heart make?
Does it sound like a chain drug through jagged rocks quake?
Does it sound like the plummet of heavy stones into a lake?
Does it sound like a trek over smoldering ashes ache?
Does it sound like the piercing shrill of an innocent animal
awake?
Does it sound like the bruising of brutality's deepest hate?
When there is no love
Left
Does it sound like a severed neck spewing?
Does it sound like a massive losing bet fight brewing?
Does it sound like unraveling reigns from a startled horse
undoing?
Or is it meek?
Does it sound like the softest folding of silk sheets?
Does it sound like the quiet whisper of dreams in sleep?
Does it sound like the willows lining the meadows that weep?
Does it sound like the deepest secret to the death that you keep?

It sounds like that
All of that
It sounds like everything
A heart breaking
Makes the noise
of the loudest suffering
A heart breaking
Is still audible
At the lowest decibel ring
A heart breaking
Cries for awareness
Because the heart is life
To all beings

What sound does a breaking heart make?
Every sound to anyone so everyone can take
In
There is a broken heart and it needs desperately to
mend

To Spring Forth

Abandoned on the coldest night
Of the longest winter ever
From the most bitter day
And didn't say a word

Laughter before languish cried
Unknown feeling inside
Never experienced an outright ditch

It was literally pain to feel
Physically ache not surreal
And the deal is that sometimes I still do wish

For you but cant surmise how anything could revise
The awful narrative of abrupt exit

Pulitzer acclaimed couldn't rewrite your heartlessness its
Shameful how do you bear name without feeling abashed

Word has it that the first will be last and the last will be first
And that means you'll catch

A glimpse of me in spring
An arise in full bloom to being the most beautiful bouquet full of life
The seed sat in earth watered by melting ice through the worst
Developing into the fairest and finest

The cold will relent the ice will repent and the spring will come
as sure as the sun
Through the coldest winter ever
we were not together
Leaving no doubt that I am the one

To Spring forth

Memory

I love your memory
It is the enemy of what came thereafter
It is a symphony of tender moments affection and
Laughter

Sweet memory
I remember in repetition
The air we shared
Endlessly in cognition
The time that you were there

Now I am here
Yet still sincere every minute we partake
In remembrances I feel your touch conversation sweet embrace

Don't ever let me go
I'll tell the next one
I should've said to you
You let me go
And all I have is the memory of us two

Together
Will we ever
Is it possible
Could it be?

Again
Will love send
Like in
My memory

Love Keeps On Loving

Love keeps on loving
Even when it's pushed away
Love keeps on loving
When it's not wanted to stay

Love keeps on loving
Even when it's rejected
Love keeps on loving
When it's not accepted

Love keeps on loving
Even through disregard
Love keeps on loving
When it's the most hard

Love keeps on loving
Even in the trying places
Love keeps on loving
When there are trials and tests and races

Love keeps on loving
Even in unflattering states
Love keeps on loving
When no other ever waits

Love keeps on loving
Even on hand and foot
Love keeps on loving
When out of sorts put

Love keeps on loving
Even in sickness sadness
Love keeps on loving
When all the world is madness

Love keeps on loving
Even when it's hated
Love keeps on loving
When it's down and underrated

Love keeps on loving
Even if not treated fairly
Love keeps on loving
When it's ominous and scary

Love keeps on loving
Even if mocked and perished
Love keeps on loving
When it's callously uncherished

Love keeps on loving
Even through winding mazes
Love keeps on loving
When scortching heat blazes

Love keeps on loving
Even at it's own risk
Love keeps on loving
When none else would do this

Love keeps on loving
Even more is required
Love keeps on loving
When it's no longer desired

Love keeps on loving
Even in absence of appreciation
Love keeps on loving
When there is no other dedication

Love keeps on loving
Even when it not reciprocal
Love keeps on loving
When waning strength is pitiful

Love keeps on loving
Even when it's shaded
Love keeps on loving
When it's power is berated

Love keeps on loving
Even in darkness and hunger
Love keeps on loving
When lightening strikes and rolling thunder

Love keeps on loving
Even in false captivity
Love keeps on loving
When counting reaches infinity

Love keeps on loving
Even through length penitentiary
Love keeps on loving
When verdicts speak endlessly

Love keeps on loving
Even in prognosis dire
Love keeps on loving
When health and wealth retire

Love keeps on loving
Even in humble reaches
Love keeps on loving
When difficult lessons teaches

Love keeps loving
Even on arctic frigid days
Love keeps on loving
When rising fog and spreading haze

Love keeps on loving
Even in altered minds
Love keeps on loving
When falling from trying climbs

Love keeps on loving
Even in present loss
Love keeps on loving
When it's needed at all cost

Love keeps on loving
Even in situations needy
Love keeps on loving
When the recipient is greedy

Love keeps on loving
Even through great travail
Love keeps on loving
When all else fails

Love keeps on loving
Even in misunderstandings
Love keeps on loving
When all else is disbanding

Love keeps on loving
Even with vision clouded
Love keeps on loving
When it's unfortunately doubted

Love keeps on loving
Even if another entices
Love keeps on loving
When it makes faithful sacrifices

Love keeps on loving
Even through all acts and deeds
Love keeps on loving
When it's case it pleads

Love keeps on loving
Even when treated poorly
Love keeps on loving
When damaged and hurting sorely

Love keeps on loving
Even to the ends of earth
Love keeps on loving
When not appreciated for worth

Love keeps on loving
Even deeply where thin
Love keeps on loving
When it's no longer welcomed in

Love keeps on loving
Even in unrecognized value
Love keeps on loving
When there is much more to do

Love keeps on loving
Even in fainter hues
Love keeps on loving
When no one else loves you

Love keeps on loving
Even in pain and strife
Love keeps on loving
When death ends and when life
. . . begins

Love is always there
Loving through right and wrong
When all hope seems lost
Love keeps loving on

Speak and Believe

Empty unto me your troubles
And I will take them away
Share with me your cares
And I will make them ok

Tell me of your dreams
and I will make them true
Tell me of your plans
There's nothing we cannot do

Speak to me your fears
And I will make them flee
Whisper to me your hopes
And I will make them reality

Listen to me
I speak
My words are just not sonnet
They live and I give
My wisdom upon it

Hear and receive
Speak and believe
Do not think like a man
Think like God
In All
Only God can

Perfect

They say nobody is
But you're Perfect
Everything about you
Is worth it
Everything about you deserves
Everything wonderful
And for everything wonderful
You're its first pick

They say there's always more
But you're the greatest
Nothing could ever replace this
Nothing you could do change the excellence of you and the
excellence of you could make all changes

They say things stay the same
But you're Outstanding
Everywhere you go you are demanded
Everywhere you've been is enhanced by everything again
Because you're everything within has commanded

They say there's nothing new
But you're the sunshine
Never did I imagine you would be mine
Never was there brighter and never could be righter than simply
you are higher than the skyline

They say there is an end
But you're forever
Lasting always because that's better
Living in hearts and minds like there is no end of time and
Love is defined when we're together

Follow Me

Follow me
I know the way
Follow me
Into the day
Follow me
Followers must be lead

I'm a leader
I'm a healer
I'm a teacher
I'm a revealer
Follow me and you all will be fed

Follow me
I am what's right
Follow me
Into the night
Follow me
Followers need a guide

I am the way
I am the truth
I am the light
Follow me I know all inside and outside

Follow me
Don't follow them
Follow me
I'll say again

Follow me
Don't let blind lead the blind
If you follow me, what you seek you will find
Follow me with your heart soul and mind
Follow me, our journey will be kind
Follow me and your pathway will shine
Follow me and do not waste your time
Following people that I have to remind
To follow me

Lost Souls Find

Where out there do lost souls look?
In the adages of the pages of every book
With expediency the ingredients of every cook
On every rack and every track and every hook

Where out there do lost souls leap?
In to the air into the sky into the deep
Into the remnants of remembrances we keep
Into the dungeons of the subjects in our sleep

Where out there do lost souls roam?
Into doors from offshores into homes
Into imaginations abscondance locations unknown
Into uncentered unfiltered quilted zones

Where out there do lost souls sing?
Into unwritten missing papering
Onto misunderstood artistic layering
Into unintelligible prophetic prayering

Where out there do lost souls find
Peace, in accepting open minds
Love, in ajar hearts throughout time
Respect, in select wisdom divine

Brave

Now at the intersection of innocence and willingness
An Edict tempered to the few
As spectacular as the bestowment of brawn embellished with the
erudite
Eschewed

Absconding to the rarity
Purely secondary the trait
Complimentary to the exemplary
tertiary chord inundates

The feeble

The weak people meet and at their consortium debate
Tries lies to surprise the demise
Of the great

Nevertheless there is no triumph
And that bitter plot
Bespecks the plotter and a daughter of the Father cannot
Be touched
Be harmed
Be reached
Be scathed

Neither the naïve
Nor the wise
Can be rebuked by the
Naive
In the absence of courage still taking action is Brave

At Least

At least from this puncture flows poetry
At least from this piercing leaks prose
At least from this abandonment a gift appeared
That I already posses and know

At last I do find closure
At length I define my present
At learning no one is deserving
Of disrupting my heaven

At lulls I hear living wisdom
At light I see His grace
At love I know very truly mine
That is never displaced

At longing I need not worry
At living I need not fret
At lasting devotion I have received
Permanent agape set

At least from this moment I capture
At least from those times I control
At least from the damage I recover
The pieces of me pure gold

And the best of me shines well told
And the rest of me remains behold
From the chest of me beats
Verses
Bold

Breathe

The sweetest sensation ever . . .

Evolved eloquently of your charming charismatic ways delicately
involved the relation of your primary secondary and tertiary
sentiments embodied in the slyest gaze upon a receptive
romantic immersed in a penchant for enamoring through a
triple layer satiated haze in remembrance of every gentle spoken
word and every silent phrase.

Presenting the most ecstatic enveloping in a ruse theatrically
modeled the extent of enchanting muse to swiftly entertain an
eternity of you,
Relaxing attracting enacting a few
Of the most amorous palatable

The most symphonic tethered . . .
Engrossed in the most ergonomic designed and tempered
together better than the depth of the diamond mining seeker,
higher than the flight of the Daedalus feather keeper, wider than
the continents epic journey reacher.

The sweetest sensation succumbed by all sensory to a breath

That I breathed when I received you and exhaled when you left.

Arrival

I have Arrived
And there is no one where i left
And no one here to pick me up

I left in anticipation
I arrived in waiting
There is never anyone

For me

But I have Arrived
And it is my dream come true
There is nobody here but me
There has never been anywhere you

I am standing on the precipice
Of all that I have dreamed
I had to go
I had to leave

I had to not worry
Who would be anywhere
Because My Arrival
Was already there.

Moonlight in the Ether

Moonlight in the Ether
That's the exclusive locale
That's the jovial playground
That is the somewhere
When no longer around

Debutante in the reverse
That's the grandiose ceremony That's the requisite retreat
That is the only date to place, placate or meet

Hindsight in the future
That's the optical illusion
That's the owning interest
That's the attractive fusion

All looking glass remembers
The visage presented parallel
The other side remits veracity
None else could tell
Or show or parlay or permit
The mirror on life acknowledges existence part of it
Is in confidence
Partially construed
When whispered to a mirror
I love you
It simultaneously says
I love you

Now imagine moonlighting in the ether
Where
Inhibitions drown
Prohibitions non-existent
Reflections abound
Reverberating sounds
Surety surrounds
Ingenuity resounds
For understanding those days and nights
When i cannot be found

Moonlighting is sweeter in the Ether
And only kindred is the Sun
To remark glorious days
Until emptying the rays
Infinitesimally undone

Enter the moon beams
Ethereally
Enlightenment
Inviting
Inspiring
Entertain
In the Ether
Believer
Believe
Be
Acclaimed

Catch Me

Catch me

I'm falling

For you

Into your arms
Its been stormy
Hold me
Keep me warm

I'm tumbling

Towards you

In constant
Unraveling
Motion

My heart is open

My arms are open

Crashing into
The ocean

Of your eyes

I saw you
Looking back at me

I'm reaching

I'm falling

I need you

To catch me

Please

I fear

I love you

I trickle down

I see the ground

Don't let me
Hit the bottom

I need you
To be around

Catch me

Watch me

Slipping through the air

Tousled

Jostled

Are you aware

I ballet

Towards you

I

Pirouette

My silhouette

Designed for you

Know that

Feel it

Traveling

Dropping

All things

Have a match

Ignited

Commend

As you extend

Your arms

To Catch

Me

There are times

There are Times
When an elevation divine
Invites the most ordinary
Intercepts and refines
Awakenings so unnatural that the disbelievers can see
The dreams of the dreamer
Manifest exactly
As time would order
And man would discover
There are times
Designed for lovers
This midnight cloak
These galaxies wrote
For a daybreak definitive
That intuition spoke
Today was ordered
A silver lined cloud bordered
A cipher of suns seeking rays
Enlightening and striking
In incommensurable ways
Just to instruct there's no luck
Only God's blessings in days
An angel awareness keeps
All of us in sleep
And hints and mentions rhymes
Some words we should heed
Some messages we need
For something special
Indeed
There are times

Thank you

In your hands right now you are holding my heart
I'm glad you're holding it so it doesn't fall apart
With your eyes right now you peer into my soul
I'm thankful that another entity can behold
To your mind right now I have written unruled

I have encountered you

. . . and you have been BEJEWELED.